W9-BRU-885

# FINGERPRINT VEHICLES

by Bobbie Nuytten

PICTURE WINDOW BOOKS
a capstone imprint

# Welcome to the fun world of fingerprint art!

Make your own digging backhoe or twirling helicopter with your fingers! Did you know that a fingerprint can be the start of a piece of art? Use the following pages to help you make your own vehicle creations!

## Here's what you'll need to get started:

### ink

Use an ink pad that's labeled washable. You can pick any size or shape you like. You can even use your favorite color!

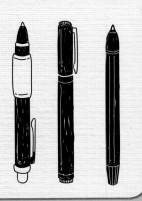

### pens

Find a pen or marker with a fine tip. An artist pen from a craft store will work too. Use the pen to add shapes and lines to your fingerprints.

### paper

Pick the paper you like best. Smooth computer paper will show the lines in your fingerprints. You can also use thicker paper from a craft store.

## FINGERPRINT TIPS

Use different parts of your finger to change the vehicle's size and shape.

Use the center of your finger or thumb to make oval shapes with lots of lines.

Use the tip of your finger to make small round shapes. Try using the side of your pinky finger for really small shapes.

Use the side of your finger to make long, skinny shapes.

Press down hard on the paper to make your fingerprint darker. A lighter touch will make your fingerprint lighter.

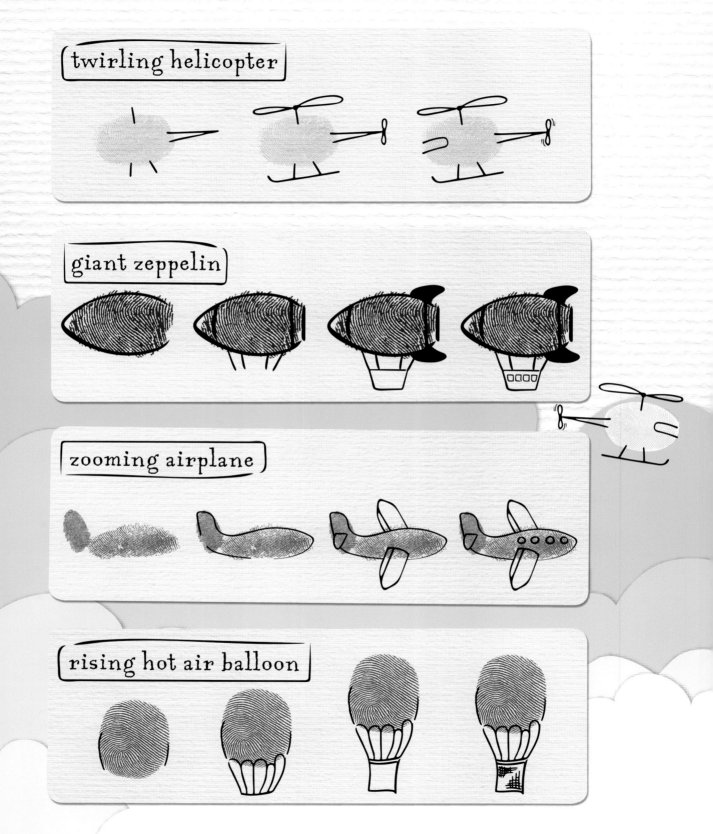

twirling helicopter

giant zeppelin

zooming airplane

rising hot air balloon

4

busy tractor

powerful grain truck

smooth skid steer loader

corny combine

flashing fire truck

speedy police car

rushing ambulance

zipping rocket

shiny UFO

roaming rover

beaming satellite

digging backhoe

hauling dump truck

lowering crane

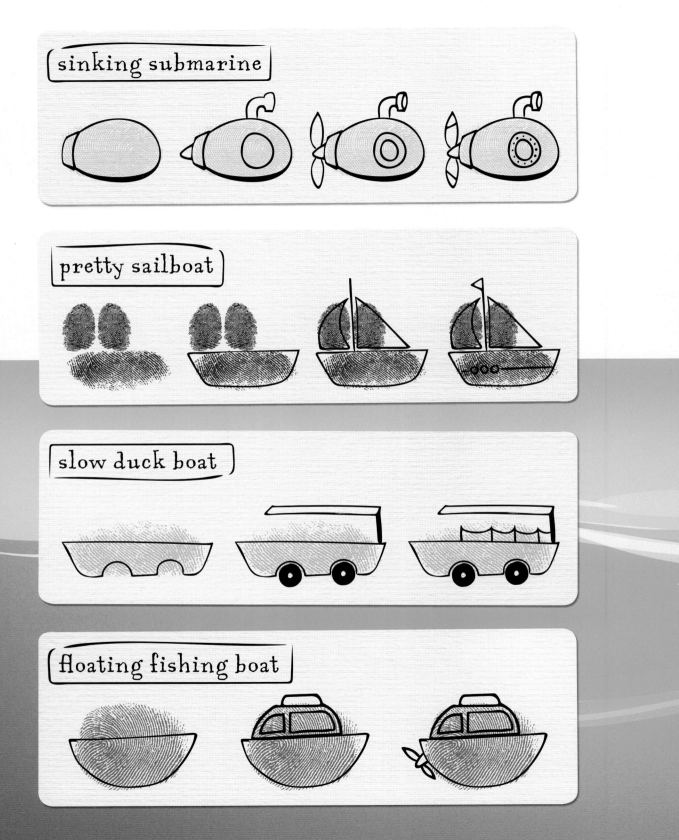

sinking submarine

pretty sailboat

slow duck boat

floating fishing boat

cruising steamship

fast race car

winning race car

pulling tow truck

16

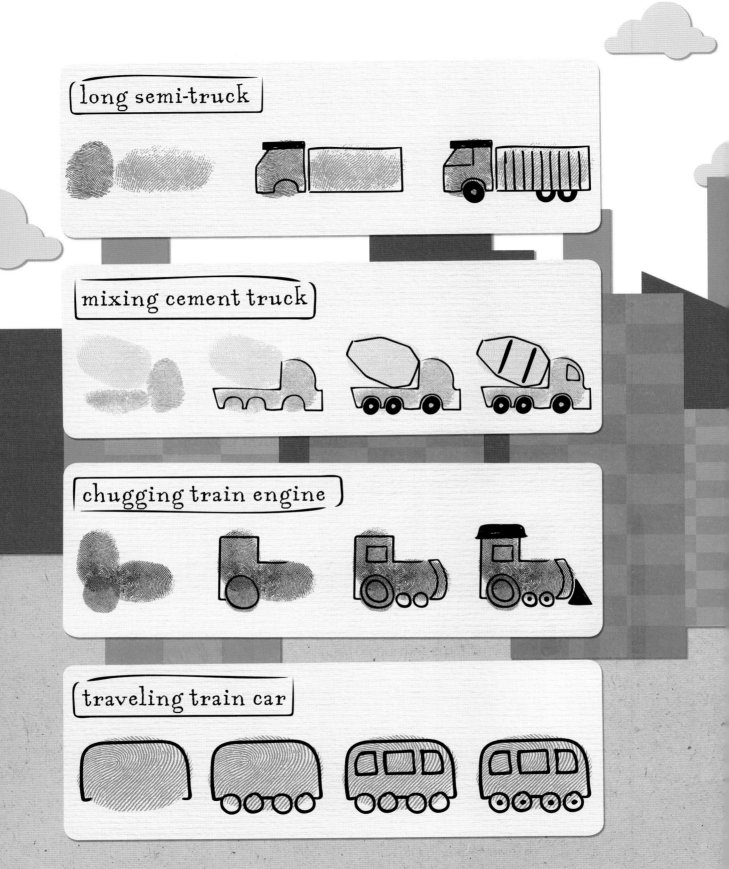

long semi-truck

mixing cement truck

chugging train engine

traveling train car

giant garbage truck

19

tough off-road vehicle

climbing dirt bike

muddy ATV

honking car

quick motorcycle

sporty convertible

speeding SUV

22

yellow school bus

*For Lexi and Mia—you taught me to see masterpieces in every scribble.*

## About the Illustrator

Bobbie Nuytten lives in southern Minnesota with her husband, two young daughters, two golden retrievers, and cat. She has been a designer for over 14 years, focusing on children's books for the last 12 years. Bobbie has always been an avid crafter. In recent years she has been interested in making art and crafts accessible and fun for kids, especially her daughters.

## Read More

**Bergin, Mark.** *Cars.* You Can Draw. New York: Gareth Stevens Pub., 2013.

**Bolte, Mari.** *Drawing Vehicles: A Step-by-Step Sketchbook.* My First Sketchbook. North Mankato, Minn.: Capstone Press, 2015.

**Cerato, Mattia.** *You Can Draw Construction Vehicles.* You Can Draw. Mankato, Minn.: Picture Window Books, 2012.

## Internet Sites

FactHound offers a safe, fun way to find Internet sites related to this book. All of the sites on FactHound have been researched by our staff.

Here's all you do:

Visit *www.facthound.com*

Type in this code: 9781479586868

 Super-cool stuff! Check out projects, games and lots more at **www.capstonekids.com**

Editor: Michelle Hasselius
Designer: Bobbie Nuytten
Creative Director: Nathan Gassman
Production Specialist: Lori Blackwell

The illustrations in this book were created with pen and ink, and digital collage.

Picture Window Books are published by Capstone,
1710 Roe Crest Drive, North Mankato, Minnesota 56003
www.mycapstone.com

**Library of Congress Cataloging-in-Publication Data**
Cataloging-in-publication information is on file with the Library of Congress.
ISBN 978-1-4795-8686-8 (library binding)
ISBN 978-1-4795-8690-5 (eBook PDF)

Photographs and background elements from Shutterstock.

Printed in the United States of America in North Mankato, Minnesota.
102015    009221CGS16

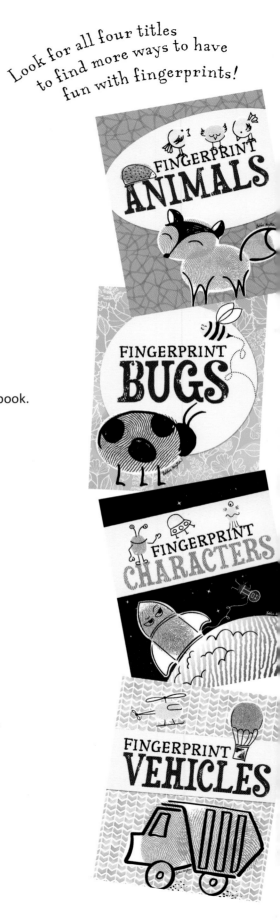

FINGERPRINT ANIMALS

FINGERPRINT BUGS

FINGERPRINT CHARACTERS

FINGERPRINT VEHICLES